Rest-of-the-Story
Short Stories

BOOK OF MONOLOGUES

Debbie E. Frederick

CROSSBOOKS
PUBLISHING

CrossBooks™
A Division of LifeWay
1663 Liberty Drive
Bloomington, IN 47403
www.crossbooks.com
Phone: 1-866-879-0502

First published by CrossBooks 9/29/2011

ISBN: 978-1-4627-0681-5 (sc)
ISBN: 978-1-4627-1040-9 (e)

Library of Congress Control Number: 2011917494

Printed in the United States of America
This book is printed on acid-free paper.

Any people depicted in stock imagery provided by Thinkstock are models,
and such images are being used for illustrative purposes only.

Certain stock imagery © Thinkstock.

Because of the dynamic nature of the Internet, any web addresses or links contained in
this book may have changed since publication and may no longer be valid. The views
expressed in this work are solely those of the author and do not necessarily reflect the
views of the publisher, and the publisher hereby disclaims any responsibility for them.

Introduction

Drama is a wonderful tool for a speaker or pastor to use when needing an object lesson or to make a good point. When you have moral or sensitive issues (i.e., purity, miracles, sin, God's transforming power), drama is a wonderful way to set the stage for what people need to hear and opens hearts to prepare for the upcoming message without being threatened or feel like they are being put on the spot.

Jesus Himself was a dramatic storyteller. These stories are designed for a relaxed setting, as well as a formal gathering or conference. Very few props are needed. The characters and their situations can be realistically portrayed by the storyteller's voice, emotion, and actions. The stories are taken from the truths of the Word with a flare of fiction woven in, as if the story could happen in modern-day times. Each character in the monologues had a face-to-face encounter with Jesus and found his or her world turned upside down. *Rest-of-The-Story Short Stories* allows the reader or story teller the opportunity to experience the situation and have the feeling of actually becoming part of the story.

Many of the attributes of Jesus Christ, our Savior and Messiah, are brought to life as the stories unfold. These include the woman at the well, the lad whose lunch fed five thousand men and their families, Anna the prophetess, and Malchus, whose ear Peter cut off. In them, Christ's love and forgiveness come through in a fresh and dramatic way.

Dedication

To my daughter Lori, who is a spirited storyteller and helped to inspire this book. Her love for the Lord and the way she brings her characters alive led me to write these stories through her eyes. Also, her love for literature and the English language helped me put them in good order. Thank you, Lori.

Contents

Acknowledgments

I truly am grateful to Dr. Patti Stoudt, who helped me with the editing of *Rest-of-the-Story Short Stories, A* Book of Monologues.

I am grateful to my husband, Steve, who inspires me to stretch and grow and use my giftings for the Lord.

How thankful I am to my Lord and Savior, Jesus Christ, for giving me the stories and for loving me when I have been unlovely and for being faithful when I am unfaithful. What a wonderful Savior!

Anna

SCENE TAKES PLACE IN THE TEMPLE.

Original text from Luke 2:36–38

I know … I'm an old woman. But I've lived a full life and served my God all my years. I'm a good Jewish woman, who comes from the tribe of Asher. God gave me a godly husband, but we were only married seven short but wonderful years before he died. I have stayed a widow all these years. Even more than that, I have stayed in the temple all this time. I spend my days in praise and worship. I practice fasting regularly and spend a lot of time in prayer.

What's that? Do I feel I missed out on life staying secluded all these years? That's a very simple answer. No, I surely don't. God and I (*Look up toward heaven*) have had an intimate relationship all through my eighty-four years. (*Smiling.*) The years have truly flown by. God has been promising me for some time that a very special event is coming, and guess what! This week it finally happened. God's son, Jesus, the Messiah, is born. The waiting is over. He has come into this world to save us from our sin. (*Speaking excitedly.*)

The prophets of old all have been telling this story a long time, and I, as a prophetess, have read and shared this story for a long, long time too, and now I was here to witness it.

Do you know His parents Mary and Joseph brought the baby Jesus here to the temple just this week? (*Open eyes wide while talking.*) I couldn't believe my eyes. When I looked into His eyes, I just knew in my heart that it was *He,* the promised Messiah. His face took my breath away. He is the most beautiful child I have ever seen, and believe me I've seen a lot of babies come to the temple through the years. (*Clasp hands and look toward heaven with a heart full of thanksgiving.*) Mary and Joseph were so proud to be His parents and dedicate Him to God.

This temple will never be the same, I promise you. There wasn't any fanfare, no dignitaries, not even one trumpet sounded upon His arrival, but yet it was the holiest and most majestic ceremony that ever took place inside these walls. (*Motion with arms around the temple.*) You could actually hear Him breathing in the reverent hush that was over the entire temple. Old Simeon got to hold Him in his arms, and when it was all over, I think it was just too much for Simeon because he asked God if he if he could die now. He said he had seen the Messiah. Not only did he see Him, he got to hold Him. If I ever were the jealous type, I think that would be one thing that would have caused me to covet. (*Wipe a tear from her cheek.*)

Yes, indeed, I am an old woman, an old woman who is also ready to go home to the Father. I have seen the Messiah! Glory to His name!

Barabbas

SCENE TAKES PLACE IN A LOCAL PRISON.

Original text from Matthew 27:15–26.

Hey, kid, slow down. What's your hurry? We're not goi`ng to no fire. These young bucks, when they gonna learn? Next thing you know, the guards will yell at 'em or, worse, they'll get a write-up. They know there's no running in the halls. You can't tell them anything. Guess they'll learn soon enough. *(Rub chin with hand in thought.)* Guess when I stop and think about it, I was just like 'em, probably worse. Nobody could tell me anything, and, if they tried, I'd just pop 'em one right on the chin. When the nice folks of town saw me coming down the street, they'd step way back till I went by, and I liked it that way. I never backed down or ran from nobody when there was trouble.

Then one day the soldiers got sick of me and threatened to lock me up and throw away the key if I didn't go with them to the judge. So, I settled down enough to go along. He never liked me, and I sure didn't have no warm fuzzy feelings for him either. As I stood there, he threw his weight around and told me

I might be thrown into the darkest hole and they would have to pump daylight down to me. That was it. I grabbed a club from one of the soldiers and gave that judge a beatin' they still talk about today. I think I heard his head crack on that last blow. At the time, I didn't care he had a wife and family at home. Soldiers came out of nowhere and it took all of them to wrestle me to the ground. They took it to me and let me have it. Then they drug me through the street and threw me in a filthy cell in the darkest part of the dungeon. I heard them makin' their *tough guy* remarks that I would never get out again, if they would even let me live. I cringed at the thought. I heard later that the judge died and the town was out for my blood.

About that time, there was some criminal everyone was all worked up over. He musta done somethin' really bad to have all town's fine people turn into a lynch mob and cry out for His blood. I remember thinkin' I wanted to meet this guy. Maybe we could hook up and teach this town a lesson or two one day. Next thing I knew, the cops were comin' right at me, carrying chains and shackles. I braced myself for the beatin' … I'd give them. They told me some guy named Pilate demanded my presence out front, so I let them shackle me and we headed out. The angry mob was really shoutin' at that criminal, so I looked over to see who He was. Sure didn't expect to see what I saw. There was this guy all bloody and battered, with some kind of matted bunch of thorns on His head.

Just as I tried to get a good look at Him, He turned His face to me and our eyes met. *(Pause.)* I felt chills run through me. *(Shudder.)* He had such a look of love, even though He was all beat up and bloody. I couldn't look away until the crowd started yellin', "Release Barabbas, release Barabbas." Whoa, that was somethin' I never heard before. And then Pilate asked what he should do with this *Jesus.* The crowd chanted all the louder, "Crucify Him, crucify Him."

I made up my mind right then I wasn't gonna stick around, in case they changed their minds. When they unshackled me, I was out of there. Yet those eyes of that Jesus feller haunted me. I knew I had to find out more about Him ... later.

So, you ask, what am I doing in this jail? *(Wave arms around room.)* Well, you see I laid low a few years, so I wouldn't draw attention to myself. After a while, I had no money and I was hungry. I decided I would kill a fine bull and cook myself a dinner. Turned out that that bull belonged to the governor's son and the boy was gettin' ready to *show* him in some big contest. They found me as I was eatin' that tasty meal outside of town and hauled me off to jail.

Guess it's good I'm here, because I started askin' about that Jesus feller, and some preacher named Peter was in the next cell for, get this, *(Leaning forward.)* telling people about that same Jesus. I couldn't believe it, so I asked him to tell me about Him.

As I listened, my heart came alive for the first time I can remember, and I actually felt hot tears running down my cheeks as I asked Him into my life.

Today? The rules don't bother me; the guards don't bother me. I'm a different man. I just tell them all about my Jesus *(Speaks with authority.)* and you know they all stop and listen!

The Woman at the Well

SCENE OPENS WITH A GREETING FROM A WOMAN STANDING IN A ROOM IN HER HOME.

Original text taken from John 4:1–42.
Props: table and chair, telephone, desk calendar.

(Cordial greeting) Welcome to my home. I'm glad you could make it. You may not know me. Over the years, I have been called a lot of things. You see me here *(Arms motion around the room.)* as I am now, a successful businesswoman, Bible teacher, and renowned storyteller. But it wasn't always like this. I guess most of us have a dark side from our past. Let me tell you about mine.

(Place hand on cheek as if thinking and recalling a thought.) I'll never forget that day. With my reputation, when it was time to go to the well for water, I didn't go when the upstanding ladies of the town went. They would go in the early morning or the cool of the evening. I always went during the heat of the afternoon. You see, I wanted to avoid their accusing eyes and their endless whispers. *(Again, think as recalling the day.)* On this particular day, there sat a man: kind eyes, a non-threatening manner, almost

welcoming me to the well. It was obvious to me that He was a Jew. I knew He wouldn't speak to me, being a woman, let alone a Samaritan. "Woman, could you get me a drink of water?" I heard him say. I looked around, startled *(Look around as if you were there.)*, wondering who He could be talking to. Then I realized … He was talking to me.

(Her phone rings, bringing her back to reality.) Hello *(Listens.)* Yes, this is she. A women's conference? *(Checking her calendar.)* You say the last weekend in April? I am free that weekend, and I would love to be a speaker. *(Pause listening.)* You get back to me with the details. Yes, I look forward to it too and will wait for your call. Good bye. *(Hangs up phone.)*

Now, where was I? Oh, yes, He asked me, a Samaritan woman, with my reputation, to get Him a drink of water. We talked awhile *(Look up as if recalling.)* and then He offered me *living water* and said I wouldn't thirst again. That intrigued me. Of course I wanted some of it, and then I wouldn't have to go to that well anymore. Then He said the strangest thing: "Go get your husband." Even that statement didn't make me feel threatened. So, I offered to Him, "I'm not married." Then you wouldn't believe what He said next. *(Throwing arms in the air.)* He said, "Yes, that's true. You've had five husbands and you're not even married to the one you're living with now." *How could He possibly have known that?* As we continued to talk, I was captivated and my heart was stirred to learn more about Him.

I did what He asked and went back to town. I started telling people about this man who told me everything I ever did. People gathered around and, as I started back to the well, the crowd moved with me, gathering more as we went, for they wanted to hear from Him too. Their hearts were also stirred. Then we all began to wonder if He might be the Messiah we heard about.

They even asked Him to stay in town a few days and continue to teach them. *(Shake head as if coming back to the present.)* Yes, friends, that was a day, yes quite a day. My life was turned upside down and I'll never be the same, nor do I want to be. *(Phone rings again.)* "Hello … yes, this is she …"

Bubba

SCENE TAKES PLACE IN LARGE
WAREHOUSE KITCHEN.
Original text taken from John 6:1–15.

Props – clipboard with papers.

Where is that shipment? *(Looking around.)* It's late. We have so much to do to get ready for the dinner tonight. All right you guys, let's not stand around. We can get the veggies cut up and two of you can peel that bushel of potatoes. Let's go, people. *(Wave arms to scatter everyone to their positions.)* Make sure the ovens are heated so when the chicken does get here, we'll be ready to get it into pans and throw them into the ovens. *(Picks up papers and looks through them.)* It looks like we'll be serving 120 to 150 people tonight. *(Tap the paper as he recalls.)* Oh, and I can't forget I invited that widow and her six children to join us too.

(Bubba begins to reflect on how he got started in his business.) Bubba's Soup Kitchen has come a long way in the past two years. Wow! I remember when I got out of culinary school a few years

ago and wanted my life to count for something important. I could open my own restaurant; maybe even a chain of Bubba restaurants. (*Hold up hands and make sign of quotes.*) I could get a loan and order the best equipment, hire and train the best employees, and I'd be ready to make a big name for myself. I might even have Bubba restaurants across the states. (*Stretch arms out to both sides.*) That somehow didn't seem like a healthy vision but more of a selfish ambition.

Then about a year ago I was invited to join a Bible study, and reluctantly I agreed to go. Somehow I would fit it into my busy schedule, but I warned them not to expect me to do anything religious. One night, as we had a discussion about our kids, a wave of memories overwhelmed me. I flashbacked to a time when I was a kid. I remember I was pacing back and forth in the kitchen begging my mamma to hurry up and pack my lunch. I didn't want to be late. When she finished it, I grabbed it and gave her a quick peck on the cheek and made a beeline out the door, slamming it as I hurried to the field outside of town. I hoped I wasn't too late. As I got closer, a huge crowd was already gathered and I wondered if I would even get close enough to hear *His* words—words that grabbed my mind and heart like a magnet, even though I was just a kid. I pushed through the crowd and tried to get up front, but everyone else wanted to see Him too. I got close enough to hear and He stood there so strongly but kindly and was saying to His close friends, "You give them something to eat."

They started out through the crowd, and one of them was walking straight at me. "Do you have any food?" he said, as he eyed the bag over my shoulder. I told him I did and he took it. He said he'd be back, and I saw him make his way back to the Master. They talked among themselves, and then I heard Master say to them, "Have the people sit down in groups of one hundred."

I found a cozy spot and watched as He opened my lunch, took out those five little loaves and two fish, and began to break them up, holding them up toward heaven. I watched them turn into *more* and *more* and *more!* I couldn't believe it. Had others given their food too? No! He only had my meager little lunch.

We all ate and ate until we were full. My stomach felt like it would burst if I ate any more. (*Patting belly.*) It was awesome! When we were done, I couldn't believe it. (*Throw up arms.*) Twelve baskets were gathered up! *How could that have happened?* When it was time to go home, I didn't want to leave, but then I raced home and told Mamma all He had said and done. She said that was nice and told me to get washed for supper. *Supper!* I was still full from all the lunch I ate.

Today, here I am with my priorities straight and life is good. I gave my heart to Jesus right there in that Bible study. I run a good soup kitchen and try to stretch my food for the many people who have little to eat, and I try to share Master's love with them as I do. That's why I'm extra excited today, because the widow I invited has a boy about the age I was when I gave the Master my lunch and later my heart. (*Sigh happily.*) All right, people, the shipment is here. Let's keep moving. We have lots to get done.

Jarius' Daughter

SCENE TAKES PLACE IN JARIUS' HOME YEARS AFTER JARIUS' DAUGHTER WAS RAISED FROM THE DEAD. JARIUS IS NOW AN OLD MAN AND LYING ON HIS DEATHBED. HIS DAUGHTER IS REMINISCING ABOUT THEIR LIFE TOGETHER.

Original text from Luke 8:40 to the end.

Props: A couch or lounge chair (not mandatory).

Oh, Daddy, it's such a joy to be your daughter. (*Stroking dad's forehead and hair.*) I love you so much, and I don't want you to die yet. We have always been so close. You have always been here for me while I was growing up and even for my own little girl now too. You always put my welfare before your own. (*Emotionally.*) You've taught me to be a good wife and mother. Thank you, Daddy. (*She pauses and looks at the ceiling, recalling the time she died and was brought back to life again.*) Wow, Daddy, do you remember the time I was so sick and you brought in so many doctors to try to make me well? I saw the fear in your eyes that I might not live.

I heard you pray for me, even when I was too sick to talk. I felt your love trying to hold on to me. Then you told me not to give up as you held me in your strong arms. (*Place your hands on your shoulders as if receiving a hug.*) You said you were going to go find Jesus, who would have the power to save me, even if no one else could. I felt my body slipping, but I also felt the excitement and hope in your hands, even though they trembled.

After you left, I tried to hold on, but I just couldn't, even with mother and others gathered around me praying. I was so weak and just wanted to go to sleep. I guess God wanted to take me home while you were gone. Somehow you found Jesus and brought Him back to the house. You told me later how He told all the family and friends to stop crying and that I wasn't dead; I was just sleeping. Everyone laughed at Him but Daddy—I can still remember that day, even though I was only twelve. I felt a strong hand take mine, and a voice said, "My child, get up." As I was waking up, at first I thought it was you with such strong hands and loving voice. (*Hold hands together as if recalling the touch.*) When I opened my eyes, (*Look up toward heaven.*) I was looking into the eyes of a wonderful loving man standing over me. I jumped up and still remember you and Mommy hugged and kissed me and everyone was amazed that I wasn't dead. You told me that it was Jesus. All my fever and sickness were gone. I knew I would trust Him the rest of my life. Mamma fixed a wonderful meal and we sat around laughing and talking while we ate, just like we knew Him all our lives.

(*She looks back to Father and smiles as she brushes a tear from her cheek.*) My, Daddy, so much has happened since that miraculous day. Do you remember how we would try to go and hear Him speak any time he was in town? There was always a large crowd gathered around Him, but we managed to get close enough to drink in all His words. When we got back home, those words burned in our hearts and we put His principles into practice in our lives. (*Heavy sigh.*)

You rest now, Daddy and get well. Just remember this. (*Touch his cheek.*) Jesus was strong enough to give me back my life, and He is certainly strong enough to give you extended life too. But … no matter what happens, we have surrendered ourselves to Him and trust Him with every part of our lives. You taught me well and prepared me to face the good and hard things in life. Jesus will walk with my family and me even after His loving arms carry you home to live with Him. I love you, Daddy. (*Bow head and sit silently for a moment.*)

The Man Healed of Demons

SCENE OPENS WITH MAN LOOKING AT
HIS REFLECTION IN THE MIRROR.

Original text from Mark chapter five.

Props: (Not required) Full-length mirror.

Look at me. My body is a mess! Strangers are afraid to look at me and turn their heads as I walk down the street. At the market, people go the other way when they see me coming through the aisles. The worst for me is when I go to the beach. I love the warm, sunny sand and the refreshing water, but I must make the others around me so uncomfortable. I know how uncomfortable *I am* when they look at all the scars on my body. (*Look down over body.*) They don't want to look, but they can't take their eyes off me. My body is repulsive to most people.

Yet, I don't *really mind the way I look too much.* (*Closes his eyes for a minute to recall his past.*) Let me tell you why. Years ago, my life

19

was full of madness. Truly it was. From the time I was a boy, I was different from other kids. I didn't have friends, because the other kids were afraid of me. The older I got, the more violent I became. I didn't want to live like that, but I couldn't do anything about it, and my own family finally was done with me too. Something would happen inside me and my body would shake as I began to run into walls or be thrown down stairs, and, even worse, I would be thrown into campfires and would be burned over and over again. I could even have died if no one was around to help me get out.

My parents didn't know what to do with me (*Throw arms up in despair.*) so they took me out of town to a deserted burial area where there were lots of caves. They told me I could live there. They said it would protect me from the town, for they wanted to stone me to death. I think they felt safer too, with me out of their everyday lives. I stayed for a while from time to time, but I got too lonely and cold, so I would go home. The same story happened time and time again. This last time, not only I but also a neighbor nearly got hurt too, so I was taken back to the caves and there I was chained like an animal! (*Dramatically.*) I was powerless to help myself. Many times I begged God to let me die. This was no way to live.

Through all my rages, my body became quite strong and people feared me all the more. I would pull on my chains until they broke under the pressure. Then I would run through the caves, bouncing off the walls, hoping each blow would be the last. It never was.

Then one day it happened. A boat arrived on shore. A man approached me, and the demons inside me began to scream at Him, "'Don't mess with me,' they said!" A war broke out in my body like no other. My body went into endless convulsions, and it drove me wild. This man asked me my name. Words came out of me, "Legion, for we are many." I felt so helpless and ashamed in front of this stranger, but He was compassionate and seemed to understand what I was going through. Those voices begged this man not to throw them into the bottomless pit. (*Thinking of that agonizing moment.*) They called this man *Jesus,* and asked Him if they could go into the pigs nearby. (*Point across the room.*) The fate of those pigs was even worse than mine (*Place hands on each side of his head, recalling it.*) and as the demons entered them, they were driven over a nearby cliff and into the water below. As I lay there catching my breath from exhaustion and pain, this Jesus was standing over me. He looked into my eyes, and such peace flowed through my body from head to toe, peace I had never felt in my life. The next thing I knew, He gave me clothes and helped me get cleaned up and gave me something to eat. At first I was afraid it might just be a dream, but His loving eyes assured me it wasn't a dream. I didn't want Him to leave me there, so I asked if I could go with Him, but He told me no (*Shaking head back and forth.*) I had to go back to town and tell my family everything that happened. I couldn't get over how good it was not to be haunted by all those evil thoughts. (*Shake as if to rid yourself of it all.*)

That's why I work here at the shelter. (*Motion around the room with arms.*) I want to give back from all the fear I put into so many people, including my parents. There are so many who come here as bad off as I was, and it makes me feel blessed to be able to help them know the love of Jesus and let them know that they too can have the hope that I found. No one is too far-gone to be restored. I'm living proof of that, scars and all.

The Woman Taken in Adultery

SCENE OPENS AS MISS REDEEMED IS TALKING WITH A NEW RESIDENT AT THE HOUSE OF HOPE.

Original text taken from John 8:3–11

Yes, dear, let's get you settled in with a nice hot bath and some clean clothes to wear. I think you'll be happy once you get settled in to the routine—here at the House of Hope. (*Point off to the right and motion up the stairs.*) The bathroom is right up those stairs and your room is down the hall on the right. Martha is waiting for you and will help you find what you need.

(*Thinking out loud.*) This place is adequate. I'm thankful we have it, but there is so much more space needed as the word gets out to women who have been abused, sold into prostitution, and those trying to break free of that lifestyle. It's also for those who have lost their way and are trying to make it back, and yes, Lord, (*Turning eyes to heaven.*) even young girls who have been scarred by men who preyed on them to make a buck or two on their innocence. (*A trace of anger and hurt show on her face.*) Yes, I could go on and on as I think of just this last year and the months and days. (*Puts her hands on her hips and looks around.*) I'm still trying to find jobs for women who are ready to step out on their own and begin to make a life for them. (*Wrings her hands in deep thought.*) And I'm trying to find homes for the younger girls who need to be part of a normal family, with a loving father and mother, without fear of being abused yet again. (*Close eyes and pray.*) Oh, Lord, give me wisdom with these precious lives and heal their hurts in Jesus' name. And, Lord, I surely thank You for sparing me and saving me that fateful day.

(*Begin to slowly pace back and forth recalling that day.*) "It was the worst *and* best day of my life. Oh, the humility and shame. The fine men of the town burst into my room (*Motion with her hands as if to push a door open.*) where I was being held down in my bed by a man who was far less than kind and had no thought for my well being. The man scooped up his clothes and ran as the town's men *grabbed me* and began to drag me out into the street. I grabbed a robe to try to cover myself as they were hurling insults while they forced me toward a crowd of people. I was thrown into the center for all to see. Even in my shame I could see they directed their loud comments to a gentle-looking man who didn't seem to belong in that scene, and they told Him I had been taken in the *very act* of adultery, and the law said I should be stoned. They asked Him tauntingly what He thought. They spoke so angrily at Him. I thought that was strange but was glad their eyes were focused on Him. He didn't say anything at first. Then He looked into my eyes and knelt down next to me and wrote in the dust of the ground.

The angry crowd kept throwing questions at Him and then He stood up. Even in my guilt and shame, I sensed a kindness I had never known. He caused a hush to go over the crowd as He said something to the effect of (*Close eyes as if trying to recall the exact words.*) "If any one of you is without sin, let him cast the first stone at her." Then He knelt down beside me again and again wrote on the ground with His finger. You could barely hear the footsteps of the men as they turned and walked away one at a time, as if they had been beaten. I was alone with my mysterious Savior. (*Pause.*) He looked into my eyes with such love, not the kind of looks I was used to getting. (*Roll eyes, knowing what she meant.*) And I felt my heart leap within me. He asked me where my accusers were and then He said those words that went straight to my heart (*Pounding chest.*) and began to heal my soul (*Throw arms up.*) even as we stood there. He said to me, "I don't condemn you either. Go and sin no more." I no longer felt cheap and dirty. I felt clean and brand new. This Jesus, my newly discovered Messiah, saved me and made me white as snow. I knew for the rest of my life I would serve Him with all my heart and life.

Now if you'll excuse me, I have an interview to conduct with a precious young woman who needs my help. Have a great day.

The Blind Man Healed

SCENE OPENS WITH A PROFESSOR AT A
UNIVERSITY FINISHING A HISTORY LECTURE AND
GETTING READY TO LEAVE THE CLASSROOM.
Original text taken from John chapter nine.

Props – books, papers, and a pair of glasses.

(*Begin gathering up papers and books.*) It was a good class today. These students are finally getting the hang of learning to think for themselves. All semester long, we have discussed historical events and the men and women who have had a part in shaping the lives of people today. It thrills my heart when I see the *light come on* as I challenge them to think outside the box. Take this week's discussion (*Remove glasses and lay them on lectern; fold hands and lean on the lectern or desk.*) on biblical history. We discussed the story of the man blind from birth, which was healed by Jesus, the One called the Messiah, the Savior of the world. We read the account in the Bible. My, did that open a can of worms! The classroom hummed with discussion, just like in the temple that day. There were many who felt the story was a farce, some felt the blind man's family sinned, and still others felt it was just a nice story. Then there was Jesus and who was he really! That certainly caused no small debate. The students were divided with some believing Jesus was the Son of God, while others thought He was an imposter.

We broke the story down step by step as I encouraged them to read between the lines of the account. I reminded them that the Pharisees felt threatened that their jobs could be on the line if they believed that Jesus was the Son of God. Also, I pointed out that the man's parents stated he *had been blind from birth,* and then realized he could *now see.* How did that happen? They were afraid they would get into trouble if they defended this Jesus, so they passed the defense to their son, and told them to ask *him* how he could see. After all, he was a grown man! Why did everyone feel so threatened, and why were they against this Jesus? As we continued, we saw the Pharisees finally confronted the man about the mysterious healing, but he stood his ground. They condemned Jesus, saying He must have been from the Devil. The healed man reminded them that God doesn't listen to bad men and summed it up by saying, "If this man were not from God, He could do nothing." That infuriated the men and they got the last word by telling him he had to be deep in sin, and how dare *he lecture them* and proceeded to throw him out of the temple!

Some of my students were negative, but several said they got the picture and saw the truth of how Jesus must have been (*Shrug shoulders.*) the Son of God. This is where I had to speak up to the class! *The story really was true.* You see, I knew all about that man. He was a direct descendant of my grandfather. As a boy, I would love to sit and listen to him telling his stories to my father and all of us. (*Pause and recall.*)

He also told us the rest of the story. Later, after he could see, that same Jesus went out and found him sitting under a tree. Jesus asked the man if he believed in Him. The man asked who Jesus was so he *could believe* in Him. Jesus said, "I am He whom you now see." Grandfather said that his grandfather of years before believed Jesus right then (*Get a little choked up.*) and began to worship Him. Jesus surely could turn darkness into light. One day, as I heard that story once again before grandfather died, I too believed. (*Emotionally.*) I shared that with my father and grandfather. We all laughed through tears of joy, as I told them I wanted to tell the world about my grandfather and his family line and about the love of Jesus. They encouraged me to go on to school so that I could study and prepare to teach others.

I cried uncontrollably at grandfather's funeral, because I knew how much I would miss Him. But I also knew he was with Jesus. I can hardly wait to be with them one day, but I know my job isn't done here. So many more need to hear the old, old story and have their eyes opened to the truth and the love of Jesus. As always, the class has a lot to think about until next week. It was definitely a good class today. (*Pick up glasses and books and exit.*)

The Woman With the Issue of Blood

SCENE OPENS WITH HOPE SITTING AT A DESK,
OPENING AN ENVELOPE CONTAINING A CHECK.

Original text taken from Luke 8:43–49.

Props: An envelope containing a paper that looks like a paycheck.

Well, look at this, my paycheck. (*Tap on the envelope.*) It surely is wonderful to have a job and be making a little money. You see, time was I had no money, no job, no hope, no anything except bills (especially doctor bills), coming in the mail. I had come to the end of myself, with nowhere to turn. I was so desperate and very sick from hemorrhaging. I didn't know what to do. Some of my friends told me to try a new doctor in town. That turned out to be another mistake and only resulted in my condition getting worse and my money gone. The loss of blood made me weaker and weaker. I tried so many doctors, and each one seemed to *experiment* on me. And then, when it was over, they would tell me they couldn't help me, but they all charged me outrageous fees. (*Place hand on heart and close eyes.*) I finally gave up. (*Shrug shoulders.*) I had no more money and was too sick and weak to fight. I really thought I was going to die. Even my friends thought there wasn't any more hope for me.

I had heard about this Jesus who the people called "The Healer." He was coming through town this very day, touching people and healing them. I cried out to Jehovah Raphah in the little strength I had left to help me and decided in my heart I would drag myself, if I had to, out into the street and wait for Him to pass by. I knew my friends wouldn't help me, because they had given up on me. I got dressed, shaking almost uncontrollably from my weakness but also with excitement, because my heart felt a final surge of hope that this Healer would be able to help me. I felt that if I could just touch His robe (*Speaking in shaking anxious voice.*) I could be healed! "Oh, Great Jehovah, hear my desperate cry!" I shouted, and with that I began the short but painful journey outside into the street, where He was due any moment. My legs gave out on me, so I crawled to a spot in the crowd where I felt I could reach Him as He walked by. There were so many people with so many needs; no one would even think I was out of place. (*Pause from weakness.*) The crowd movement intensified and people were pushing at each other to be out in front to see this one they were calling "Messiah" and "Healer." I feared I would be trampled, but this was my last hope. I held my position. He was coming. I inched even closer so I could brush His robe, and I just made it … as He tried to press on through the crowd.

Just as I touched Him, He stopped right there in the middle of throngs of people. He turned … and spoke these words: "Who touched me?" Those with Him looked at each other in amazement that He would ask that! A man named Peter, I believe, said, "Master, people are crowding and pressing against You. How can You ask that?" I got really scared, and yet I could feel I was regaining my strength. (*Excitedly.*) I was being healed! (*Pause.*) Then He said, "Someone touched me and I felt my strength go out of me. Someone has been healed today."

I was at His feet, and knew I had to speak up and tell Him it was I. There, in front of everyone, I blurted out my story, and all could hear it. When I was done, He looked at me with compassion and great love (*Point to self.*) and said, "Daughter, your faith has healed you. Go in peace."

Peace did pour over me from head to toe. No one knows how my heart rejoiced as I felt strength and wholeness rush through my body. It had been more than twelve years since I was strong and healthy. I leaped for joy and hurried home. I had been healed. (*Excitement in her voice intensifies.*) That Healer gave me back my life. I vowed that I would serve Him the rest of my days.

So, you can see why this paycheck is so important. (*Holding it up.*) Today I am an assistant to a team of doctors who study blood diseases, *and* I also organized a prayer team. We pray for the sick that come to us, first for their salvation and then for their healing. I am so blessed to be used by the King of Kings, my Savior and my Healer. Do you know how much He loves you too? My friends, I pray you too will come to know Him and His great love for you. Nothing is impossible with God.

Simon of Cyrene

SCENE TAKES PLACE ON THE ROAD TO JERUSALEM.

Original text taken from Mark 15:21–24.

My day started normal enough. I got up early that morning, ate a quick breakfast, and started my trek to Jerusalem. I wanted to get into town and back before all that religious stuff would take place. I never got involved, but lots of my neighbors wouldn't miss it. I didn't really want to go, but had no choice. My plow broke, and I wanted to get the last of the seed in the ground before the rain would come. Off I hurried, and it was strange that, as I was heading into town, the people there seemed either silent and sad or arrogant and angry. This was not what I would have expected, today of all days.

Just about that time, everything broke loose. There was such chaos and frenzy, and I didn't understand it. I just couldn't figure it out. At first I thought a parade was coming because the people were lined up on both sides of the road. But, as I looked closer, there were soldiers with whips lashing out at three men carrying crosses of all things. What kind of religious act was this? The soldiers were whipping them and screaming at them to keep moving, heading out of town. It was a pitiful sight, so I stepped out of the way. The first two went by, and one of the two was cursing right back at the soldiers as they wailed him with their whips. He did this even under the weight of the cross. I was shocked at the third man, who was bloody from head to toe and had some kind of hideous crown on His head. The brutal soldiers seemed to love to strike Him extra hard, causing blood to pour from His head, back, and everywhere on His body!

I'm no small man and really couldn't get lost in the crowd to see what was going to happen. Just about then, that poor soul simply collapsed (*Motion body as if the body crumbled to the ground.*) under the weight of the cross and the brutality of the beating he was enduring. He just lay there and didn't respond to the cursing and lashing the soldiers continued crashing on Him. Now they were really angry, and looked up at the crowd. I knew it. They spotted me standing there. One of them screamed at me, "You, yeah, you! Come here and help carry this cross." I wanted nothing to do with it, but one of them threatened me with his whip, so reluctantly I walked over to Him. I took hold of the cross easily with one hand and then reached to this poor wretch and helped Him to His feet with my other hand. He was so weak in His body, but as I steadied Him and looked in His eyes through all the blood, He showed a powerful strength and love that poured from His eyes as much as the blood from His wounds. It made me feel stronger just from His looking at me. His blood was all over the cross, and as I threw it on my back, I felt some drip on my cheek. He quietly whispered, "Simon, this blood is for you too." What in the world was He talking about? I didn't want His blood. *How did He know my name?*

The soldiers started heckling again, so I quickly began to walk with Him. This man, I knew there was something about Him that I never knew in anyone else. The people who loved Him and were along the road kept calling Him "Jesus, Messiah." I had heard about Him, but I never dreamed I would help *Him* carry a cross. Stranger still, my mind kept playing tricks on me, making me think He was helping *me*. Who was this man?

We arrived on a hill outside the city, where I couldn't wait to be rid of that cross and try to shake the power that Jesus had on me. I lingered behind in the crowd to watch what would happen next. I saw those soldiers place His battered body on the cross and then they pounded spikes through His hands and feet and into the splintered tree. *Why? What had He done so wrong* to deserve to die like this? He hung there in agony. I couldn't watch any longer. As I started to walk away, I heard Him say, "Father, forgive them, for they know not what they do." Somehow guilt rose up inside me, as if I had nailed Him to that tree! I knew that night as I thrashed about in bed, unable to sleep, that I had to find out from someone how that one man could turn the world *and* my life upside down. Could He actually be ... the Messiah?

Malchus the Soldier

SCENE OPENS AT MALCHUS' HOME.
Original text taken from John 18:1–11.

My head was pounding as I tried to lie down and go to sleep. I liked my job, and it paid the bills. I had steady work and my family didn't want for anything. But this weekend, man, I shudder as I recall all I had seen and experienced. I never want to go through another weekend like the one I just had. Yet I now knew God had a plan for my life, and that made it all bearable.

Thursday started out like any other. I had breakfast with my family, kissed my wife good-bye, ruffled the hair on my sons' heads, and then went off to work. When I got there, we had no specific orders but were told to be ready for trouble that might be ahead later in the day. We talked among ourselves and agreed that that usually meant there could be a riot brewing or a famed criminal was going to be captured or was going to be put to trial. A certain amount of excitement rose up in me, but then I thought of my family and how they counted on me.

A few small problems came up, but nothing big until a meeting was called and we were summoned to go bring in a criminal for questioning. We armed ourselves and started out to find Him. It was getting late, so we got torches to light the way. We were told He would be with His gang in the garden. I thought that was a strange place for criminals to gather. As we walked and talked, we were warned He could be dangerous. When we arrived, a man, asking who we were looking for, met us. Our commander said, "Jesus the Nazarene," to which He responded, "I am He." (*Shock.*) We all dropped back in amazement. This certainly wasn't a greeting we were expecting! Then He asked us again. And again, we said we were after Jesus. The commander had a civilian with him who stepped out and went up to Jesus and kissed Him. That blew my mind, as I was the servant of the high priest. We certainly never kissed each other. I learned later that the kiss that man received was a kiss of betrayal. They exchanged words that I couldn't hear. One of Jesus's men grabbed a sword and swung it right at me, slicing off my right ear. Jesus picked it up, and, before I could move, that guy put it against my head and it was completely healed, as if it never happened. Did it really happen? I have no effects or scar to say it did, except the blood on my uniform and the gnawing pit in my stomach.

That was just the kickoff of a nightmare night! He was bound and we took Him in, where He was questioned over and over. He never opened his mouth to defend Himself, except to say he was Jesus. We were asked to work overtime and escort this prisoner from one official to another, but it seemed like no one wanted to deal with Him, almost as if they were afraid of Him. He certainly wasn't a typical prisoner. When He healed my ear, I couldn't avoid His eyes, eyes that pierced into my heart like that sword with my ear. I couldn't shake that look. (*Shake head.*) When we finally took him to Caiaphas, we were discharged and I went home, totally shaken by the night's events.

The next morning I went to work, anxious to hear what had happened to the prisoner. Things were still in such turmoil. They were preparing to execute three men, and Jesus was one of them. *Why?* I didn't dare ask, for it could mean my job or, worse, my life, the way things were going. I was chosen to help with crowd control, so I stayed as close as I could to Jesus to see what would happen. He had been beaten so badly, I wasn't sure it was He carrying that cross, until He looked into my eyes along the road. Then I knew. We arrived at Skull Hill, where all three were nailed to the crosses they were carrying and then displayed for all to see that this is what you do to criminals. Jesus was in the middle. I felt such guilt as I watched Him suffer the shame and agony. I wanted to take Him down and help Him as He helped me. When He cried out, "It is finished," my heart felt as though a sword had been thrust through it. Somehow I knew my life wasn't finished, but just beginning. I couldn't explain it (*Pointing to chest.*) but I had to find out more about him. I was determined to find someone who could help me sort through all this. Sunday morning came and His body disappeared. That created even greater havoc. I overheard some women nearby say that Jesus had risen from the dead. I felt such joy that He was alive, but did He really rise up from the dead? (*Then turn from joy to questions.*) When will I find out more about Him?

Elizabeth

Well, my time is running out. My old bones are worn down, and I can't get around anymore. Oh, but my heart is full. I can barely see either, but the joy in my soul is complete. Old Zach and I have had such a good life together. When we were younger, we felt we could conquer the world together. He was a priest in the temple and we sure spent a lot of time there praying. (*Thinking out loud.*) I used to wonder what he did when he went into the most holy place. Sometimes when he came out of there, I knew by his face he had been in the presence of the Almighty. He just radiated such a holy aura it would almost scare me. As much as he loved me, I could see he loved his Lord all the more.

You know we didn't have children through all our married years and I would cry in his arms many nights. God has always been so good to us every other way. Why didn't He grant us children? All my friends were having babies. They always shared their stories of how they would have to get up in the night to feed and take care of crying babies when they were sick or hungry. I felt such emptiness as I would listen to them share the good and bad experiences and I could hear the laughter that rang through their tents. (*Pause as if recalling the pain and empty feeling of being barren.*) My tent was always silent and void of any children's laughter or cries.

This went on for years. I would cry out to the Lord in the temple, and I thought He heard me. But month after month, year after year, my prayers were never answered. I had pretty much given up any hope, especially when I got too old to bear babies anymore. "Why, Lord, why?" I would cry out in the middle of the nights when I could have been humming while nursing a child. "Just one child, Lord, couldn't you grant Zach and me one child?"

It seemed it fell on deaf ears. Until one day I was baking bread and Zach came home from the temple. Something was wrong. When I asked what happened, he couldn't speak. He had lost his voice. You see, he had a visitor in the holy place and the visitor told him God heard our cries and we would have a son and we were to call him John. When Zach asked how that could possibly happen when we're both way too old, the visitor said he was Gabriel and had stood in the presence of God, Who sent him to us to share the good news. He also said that because Zach doubted, he would not be able to speak. He had to write all this down for me. I couldn't believe my eyes, but, sure enough, the words were true. God opened my womb and I conceived a son. Now he's growing up way too quickly.

I'm so very tired and my time is running out, but let me tell you the best part of my story. When I was six months along, my young cousin Mary came to visit me. She told me she had news for me. Well, when that little baby inside of me heard Mary's greeting, it leaped for joy in my belly. I was so overwhelmed that when the Holy Spirit came over me, I couldn't help but cry out, in a loud voice mind you, "Blessed are you among women, and blessed is the child you will bear! Why am I favored that the mother of my Lord should come to me?" I told Mary how the baby leaped in my womb at the sound of her voice. She stayed with Zach and me right up until the time for baby John to be born.

I am too weak to go on. (*Pause.*) I do feel bad that I won't see the rest of John's life, but I am quite sure he and Mary's son Jesus, (*Point to chest.*) my Messiah, will bring honor to God. My joy is complete.

About the Author

Debbie E. Frederick is a married mother of five children, eleven grandchildren, and one great-grandson. Her life has been a roller coaster ride, but Christ has been the anchor through it all. Many of her life experiences were previously chronicled in *Pearls in Due Season,* co-written by Frederick and her husband, Steve.

CPSIA information can be obtained at www.ICGtesting.com
Printed in the USA
BVOW070705111011

273303BV00002B/4/P

9 781462 706815